BOSTON'S FREEDOM TRAIL

BOSTON'S FREEDOM TRAIL

DILLON PRESS
New York

Maxwell Macmillan Canada
Toronto
Maxwell Macmillan International
New York Oxford Singapore Sydney

By *Terry Dunnahoo*

To my grandson Brendan,
with love

Photo Credits

United States Department of the Interior (National Park Service): pages 2-3, 22-23, 25, 27, 31, 33, 35, 36, 37, 39, 40, 43, 53, 54-55, and 59

The Bettmann Archive: pages 6, 15, 19, and 48

Library of Congress Cataloging-in-Publication Data

Dunnahoo, Terry.
    Boston's freedom trail / by Terry Dunnahoo. — 1st ed.
      p. cm. — (Places in American history)
    Includes index.
    ISBN 0-87518-623-8   0-382-24762-0 (pbk.)
    1. Freedom Trail (Boston, Mass.)—Guidebooks—Juvenile literature. 2. Boston (Mass.)—History—Colonial period, ca. 1600-1775—Juvenile literature. 4. Boston (Mass.)—History—Revolution, 1775-1783—Juvenile literature. [1. Freedom Trail (Boston, Mass.)—Guides. 2. Boston (Mass.)—History.] I. Title. II. Series.
    F73.37.D86   1994
    917.44'610443—dc20   94-470

Summary: Describes the area in Boston where historically significant events such as the Boston Tea Party, Boston Massacre, and Paul Revere's famous ride took place.

Dillon Press   Maxwell Macmillan Canada, Inc.
Macmillan Publishing Company   1200 Eglinton Avenue East
866 Third Avenue   Suite 200
New York, NY 10022   Don Mills, Ontario M3C 3N1

Macmillan Publishing Company is part of the Maxwell Communication Group of Companies.

First edition

Printed in the United States of America

10 9 8 7 6 5 4 3 2 1

CONTENTS

1. Boston and Bullets...7

2. A Tea Party and a Codfish............................17

3. Mother Goose and a Grasshopper........................29

4. Spies and a Midnight Ride...............................42

5. The Whites of Their Eyes.................................52

Visitor Information..60

Historical Time Line..62

Index...64

A painting of Paul Revere's famous ride

CHAPTER 1

BOSTON AND BULLETS

Listen, my children, and you shall hear
Of the midnight ride of Paul Revere,
On the eighteenth of April, in 'Seventy-five;
Hardly a man is now alive
Who remembers that famous day and year.

Thousands of children have learned the above words. They are the first lines of "Paul Revere's Ride," a poem written by Henry W. Longfellow. The poet used his imagination to make his words rhyme and to make Revere's ride sound even more exciting. But the trip from Boston to Lexington on April 18, 1775, *was* more exciting than the rider wanted it to be.

At about ten o'clock that morning, two of

Revere's friends sneaked him past armed guards so he could warn people that the British were ready to attack. Soldiers were everywhere. After they captured Paul Revere, they held a gun to his head.

On Boston's Freedom Trail, you can learn about Paul Revere's ride and about his capture. You can even see the house he lived in, the house that he left the night he rode through the countryside to warn the people in Boston that the British were coming to attack them. You can see where people were shot during the Boston Massacre and where the Boston Tea Party took place.

All this happened in the 1770s. But not everything on Boston's Freedom Trail is about the 1770s. There is also an interracial monument to honor people who fought in the Civil War. And the USS *Constitution*, the oldest ship in the U.S. Navy, is docked at the Charlestown

Navy Yard. The ship was used to help win the
War of 1812. You can go aboard the *Constitution*
and pretend you are the captain of the ship.

The history you will learn on the Freedom
Trail began when colonists sailed from England
in 1630 and settled in Boston. They sailed 3,000
miles across the Atlantic Ocean to build a settle-
ment they called Charlestown. They soon
learned there was not enough water to cook or
farm with or to drink. Many people moved across
the Charles River. Since some settlers had come
from a city in England called Boston, they named
their new town Boston. In 1632 Boston became
the capital of the Massachusetts Bay Colony.

More colonists crossed the Atlantic. Some
made money by building ships. Some people
made hats and shoes. Others farmed or fished.
Apollos Rivoire, a silversmith, opened a shop. He
changed his name to Revere and called his son
Paul.

For a while, the king of England was too

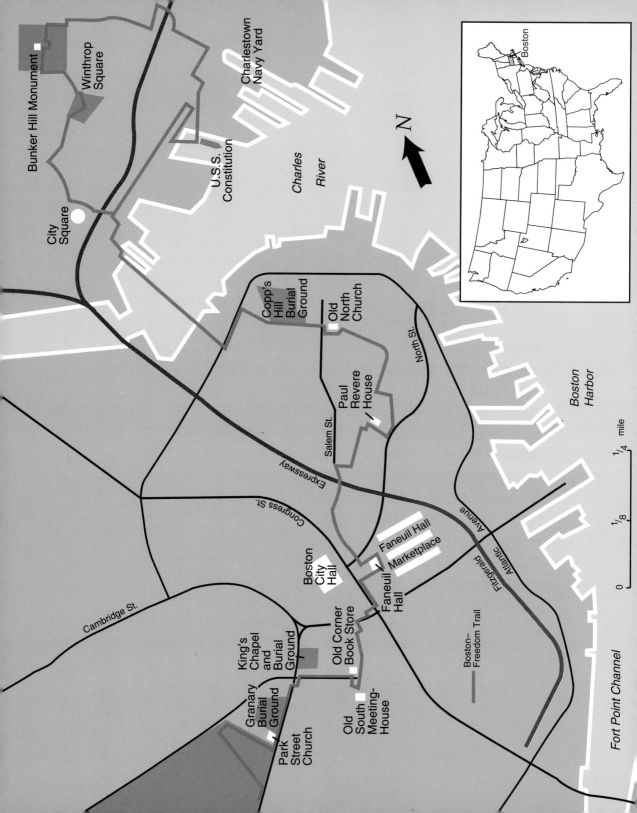

Bunker Hill Monument

Winthrop Square

Charlestown Navy Yard

U.S.S. Constitution

Charles River

City Square

N

Boston

Copp's Hill Burial Ground

Old North Church

North St.

Boston Harbor

Paul Revere House

Salem St.

Expressway

Congress St.

Fitzgerald Avenue

Atlantic

Faneuil Hall Marketplace

Boston City Hall

Faneuil Hall

Cambridge St.

Old Corner Book Store

King's Chapel and Burial Ground

Granary Burial Ground

Park Street Church

Old South Meeting-House

Boston— Freedom Trail

Fort Point Channel

1/4 mile

1/8

0

busy fighting wars to bother with the colonists. But when he ran out of money, he asked the colonists for more taxes. Many settlers said they already paid too many taxes. These people called themselves patriots. Other colonists who were loyal to the king called themselves Tories.

As time passed, it seemed the king stayed awake nights thinking of ways to take money from the colonists. Riots often broke out. On October 1, 1768, soldiers were sent from England to keep peace in the colony. People watched them march to Boston Common, where they pitched their tents. Other soldiers went to Faneuil Hall in Boston, where patriots often met to talk about how to get rid of the never-ending taxes.

More soldiers came on November 10. They were always yelling orders. They stopped people, too, especially after the nine o'clock curfew. That was when a bell warned people to put out their candles. The town crier walked through the dark, twisting streets, calling the time and weather.

Patriots liked to taunt the soldiers. Sometimes they threw eggs and rocks at them, and the soldiers threatened to fight back. Nothing serious happened, however, so some soldiers went back to England. The king made Thomas Hutchinson governor of the colony. Hutchinson was a Tory born in Boston, and he thought he was the only kind of person who could rule Boston.

Patriots did not like the governor's thinking. They did not like store owners who bought things from England. Patriots asked people not to go into these stores, but some people went in anyway. Boys threw dirt, oyster shells, and garbage at them. On February 22, 1770, during such an incident, gunfire exploded. Bullets hit 11-year-old Christopher Snider in the chest and stomach. People streamed from their houses to see what had happened. The men who had killed

Christopher were put in jail.

Four days later, six young boys carried Christopher's coffin through the snow to the Granary Burying Ground. Two thousand people and 30 carriages followed down King Street. The street was usually filled with the noise of children playing, peddlers yelling from their carts, and wagons heading for the wharf. But on that day, only the rhythm of the horses' hooves on the cobblestones broke the silence.

After Christopher's death, fights broke out everywhere. The worst was at the Custom House on March 5, 1770. A barber thought a British officer had not paid for his haircut, and he told an apprentice to get the money. The apprentice caught up with the officer at the Custom House and tried to talk to him. But a soldier hit the apprentice with his musket, and the man staggered away, bleeding.

A crowd surrounded the soldier as church bells warned of trouble. Some people thought the bells meant there was a fire. They grabbed their leather buckets and went looking for it. When they did not see anything burning, most people headed for the Custom House to see what was going on.

The soldier was ducking snowballs and chunks of ice. Then he called for help, ran up the steps, and loaded his musket. Captain Thomas Preston heard him and led seven soldiers to the Custom House. The crowd, jeering and yelling, closed in and challenged the soldiers to fire.

Then a man named Crispus Attucks threw a stick. A soldier fell and dropped his musket. There was a fight for the gun, and the soldier retrieved it. He aimed at people yelling "fire."

A soldier fired his musket. Crispus Attucks fell. Other soldiers opened fire, and Captain Preston ordered them to stop. Three men lay dead, and blood from eight others turned the snow red. Two of the wounded men later died. People scattered, but a few carried away the

The Boston Massacre. Crispus Attucks, at the right, lies wounded.

dead and wounded men. When Captain Preston asked his men why they'd fired, the soldiers said they thought he had ordered them to do it.

Once again people gathered for a funeral, about 4,000 this time. Separate hearses for the five men headed for the Granary Burial Ground. Two days later, Patrick Carr, one of the wounded men, was near death. A doctor asked the man if the crowd had abused the soldiers. Carr said he was surprised the soldiers had not fired sooner. Captain Preston and six of his men were found innocent. The other two were found guilty.

Paul Revere, who'd become a silversmith like his father, made an engraving depicting this incident and called it "Bloody Massacre." There were mistakes in the engraving. The most obvious was the time shown on the Custom House clock. The first prints showed 8:00. On other prints, Revere changed the time to 10:25, which was closer to the time of the Boston Massacre.

CHAPTER 2

A TEA PARTY AND
A CODFISH

Some people believed the Boston Massacre happened because a group of people had broken the law. Others believed it was time to fight harder for freedom from England. The patriots had caused so much trouble that the king got rid of all taxes except the one on tea. He thought the colonists would be happy about this. But they said that if they paid the tax, it would mean the king had the right to tax them. He did have the right, but patriots believed that not paying taxes was a giant step toward freedom.

The British ships *Dartmouth, Eleanor*, and *Beaver*, each filled with tea, sailed into Boston harbor. The patriots gave Governor Hutchinson a deadline, December 16, 1773, to send back the tea. When that day arrived, the ships were still in the harbor. Patriot leaders went to the governor's house to give him one last chance to send back the tea. He refused.

Then patriots disguised as Indians hurried to Griffin's Wharf, their faces covered with soot, paint, and charcoal. They were dressed in anything they thought Indians would wear, including blankets.

The men had been warned they would be tried for treason if they were caught. But they shrugged off the warning. At the wharf they separated into three groups, led by Samuel Adams, John Hancock, and Paul Revere. While the men dumped the 340 chests of tea, nobody laughed or joked. This was not a party; this was a protest.

Orders had been given to leave the ships the way the patriots found them, so after the men finished dumping the tea, they swept the decks and docks. Then every man took off his shoes and turned out his pockets to make sure every

An engraving that shows the Boston Tea Party

speck of tea went into the water. One man was thrown overboard when he stuffed tea into his pockets. When the protest was over, Paul Revere rode his horse to Philadelphia and New York to tell other colonists the news.

Patriots were questioned, but nobody talked. The British punished the colonists with the

Boston Port Bill. No ship was allowed to enter the harbor after June 1, 1774, until the patriots had paid for the tea. The bill also allowed British officials to search the colonists' homes for smuggled goods. Then came the final blow. More soldiers arrived with General Thomas Gage as their leader.

People in the other 12 colonies also had tax problems, so they had not been able to help the Massachusetts Bay Colony. But when the harbor closed, towns sent rye and flour. Wagons rumbled in from South Carolina with rice. Maryland sent wheat. People in Boston were often hungry, but they did not give in to the king's orders.

On September 5, 1774, the First Continental Congress was held in Philadelphia. Leaders from 12 colonies came, including Samuel Adams and John Hancock. (Georgia did not send a representative.) The delegates could not make laws, but they did send a Declaration of Rights and Grievances to England. The king ignored the colonists. When they met again on May 10, 1775, for the Second Continental Congress, the king could no longer ignore them. Minutemen and British soldiers had already fought at Lexington and Concord.

When you visit Boston's Freedom Trail, go into Paul Revere's house and walk through the Common, where British soldiers camped. The Common is the best place to begin your tour. People at the information booth will answer your questions and tell you about "the red line." It begins at the Common and ends at Bunker Hill.

Sometimes the line is painted on the sidewalk. Sometimes the line is red brick in the sidewalk. And, just to keep you on your toes, sometimes the trail is marked by gray stones on a red brick sidewalk. If you follow the red line the way Dorothy followed the Yellow Brick Road in the *Wizard of Oz*, you will see the history of Boston.

The Common is the oldest public park in the

An aerial view of Boston's Common, the park where the Freedom Trail begins

United States. When the colonists moved from Charlestown to Boston, this area was common land, which meant it belonged to everyone. The Common was used to graze cattle and also as a place to punish criminals, pirates, and witches. People who swore had their heads and wrists put in pillories. And there was a ducking stool at the edge of Frog Pond to punish wives who nagged their husbands.

From the information booth, follow the red line to the Massachusetts State House. In 1795, 15 white horses pulled the cornerstone up Beacon Hill. Three years later, the State House opened. You can take a tour of the building. Look for the life-size wooden codfish in the House of Representatives. It was hung there to show how important codfish were to the Massachusetts Bay Colony, especially after the king had closed Boston harbor.

Shingles were used to cover the dome of the building, but they leaked. In 1802 copper was

The Massachusetts State House, on Boston's Beacon Hill

put on. After the Civil War, the dome was gilded with gold. It was especially beautiful when the sun or moon reflected on it. During World War II, the dome was painted gray because the United States government worried that enemies might use it to find Boston in the dark and bomb the city. The dome is now gilded with gold again.

In 1634, a skillet filled with tar was put on a pole at the top of the hill. If enemies attacked Boston, somebody was supposed to climb the pole and light the tar to warn people. When tension between patriots and the British increased, another beacon was put up. The beacons were never used.

Opposite the State House is an interracial monument to honor those who fought during the Civil War. When war broke out in 1861, African Americans were not allowed to fight. They finally got permission to do so, but not as officers. Colonel Robert Gould Shaw volunteered to lead the 54th Massachusetts Regiment.

Opposite the State House: Robert Gould Shaw's memorial celebrating the 54th Massachusetts Regiment

If the soldiers were captured, they would become slaves again. If Colonel Shaw was captured, he would be called a traitor to his race. And there was the danger of being killed in battle. This happened to the colonel and 32 of his soldiers. They died while attacking Fort Wagner in South Carolina. They were buried together at the fort.

The interracial monument is part of the Black Heritage Trail. This trail celebrates the achievements of Boston's African American community between 1800 and 1900 on Beacon Hill. Some sites can be visited independently, but others may be seen only as part of a tour.

MOTHER GOOSE AND A GRASSHOPPER

Not far from the Black Heritage Trail is Park Street Church. During the War of 1812, members of the church worried that gunpowder stored in the crypt would blow them up. They called the church Brimstone Corner.

Next door is Granary Burying Ground. Benjamin Franklin's parents and other members of his family are buried there. He is buried in Philadelphia. Samuel Adams, Paul Revere, and John Hancock are also in that cemetery. Not far from Hancock's grave is a stone marked "Frank, servant to John Hancock Esq." Frank died in 1771, and since there is no last name on the headstone, it is thought that he was probably John Hancock's slave.

Some people believe "Mother Goose" is buried in this cemetery. The woman known as Mother Goose was Elizabeth Vergoose. She was married to Isaac Vergoose, a man who already had ten children. Then Elizabeth and Isaac had ten children together. With twenty children and dozens of grandchildren, Elizabeth sang a lot of nursery rhymes. In 1719 her son-in-law Thomas Fleet published "Songs for the Nursery." People started calling Mrs. Vergoose Mother Goose. But long before her work was published, children sang rhymes. So perhaps there was more than one Mother Goose.

As you walk through the cemetery, you will see the name of Isaac Vergoose's first wife. But you will not find Elizabeth's gravestone. It disappeared years ago. Maybe someone thought she was the real Mother Goose and took the gravestone for a souvenir.

The oldest cemetery in Boston is King's Chapel Burial Ground. It was used almost from

The King's Chapel Burial Ground

the day the first colonists came to Boston. By the 1740s, so many people were buried there that grave diggers complained they had to bury the dead four deep. William Dawes, who, with Paul Revere, rode by land to Lexington to warn that the British were coming, is buried in this cemetery.

In 1687 Tories took part of the cemetery to build King's Chapel. When the cornerstone for a larger church was put down in 1749, patriots cursed the British for disturbing the dead. In 1754, to make the church bigger, the British knocked down Boston Latin School, the first school in that city, built in 1645. Samuel Adams, Benjamin Franklin, and John Hancock attended that school. The mosaic hopscotch you see in the pavement shows where the school stood.

Nobody knocked down the Old Corner Book Store. It was built in 1712, after a fire burned most of this part of Boston. Many authors and poets, including Longfellow, who wrote about Paul Revere's ride, met in the store to write and talk about their books.

Not everybody could read. Many shops had signs over their doors to show what was sold inside. A cobbler had a sign with a boot. A tailor

Boston's Old Corner Book Store

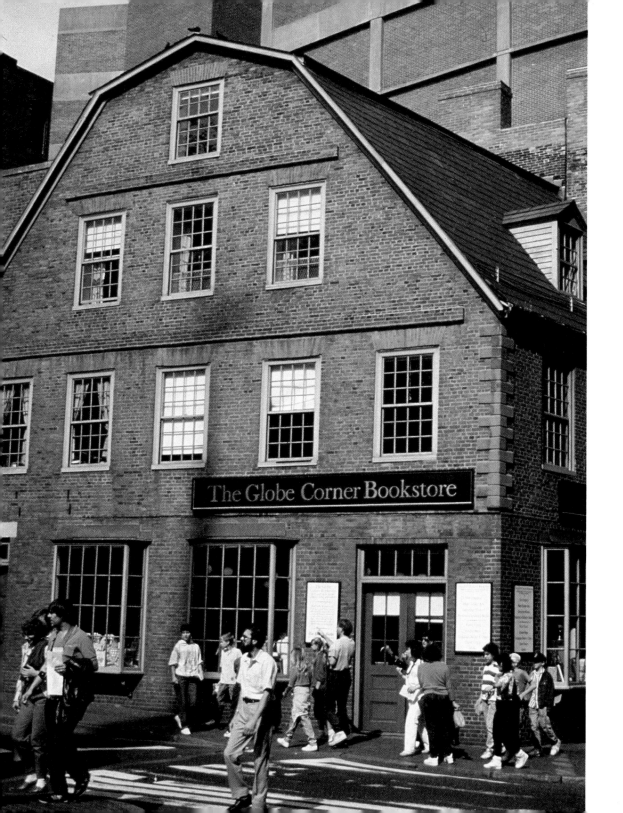

may have had a sign with a needle and thread, or maybe a pair of scissors. People who sold meat put animal heads on their signs.

But even people who could not read knew that butchers sold meat. That was because carcasses hung from hooks for everyone to see. Dogs would jump to get at the meat they could not reach. In 1728 a law was passed that said dogs in Boston could be no taller than ten inches high. Before the law, dogs were always biting off chunks of meat. Sometimes the really big dogs ran off with whole carcasses. Even after the law was passed, Samuel Adams kept an enormous dog, a Newfoundland, but nobody dared tell Adams to get rid of the animal.

The next stop on the Freedom Trail is the Old South Meeting-House. While Tories worshiped at the King's Chapel, patriots prayed at the Meeting-House. During the Revolutionary War, British soldiers burned the Meeting-House pulpit, pews, and prayer books and used the

The Old South Meeting-House

The Old State House, in the 18th century (above) and as it appears today (right). It is the oldest public building in Boston.

building for stables and a riding school. After the British were chased out of Boston, the building was used as a church again. Now it is a museum, where you can see how people lived during those early days.

Close by is the Old State House. It was the capitol of the Massachusetts Bay Colony until the new State House was built on Beacon Hill.

The king's governor and other royal officials ran the government from the Old State House. The Massachusetts Assembly, elected by the people, met there, too. The patriots and Tories argued a lot. When new laws from England were read from the balcony, patriots jeered.

But on July 18, 1776, there were cheers, not jeers. That was the day Colonel Thomas Crafts read the Declaration of Independence from the balcony. That night, patriots celebrated with a bonfire in the square and burned anything that reminded them of the British. Today, below the balcony, you can see a circle of paving stones that mark the place where Crispus Attucks was shot during the Boston Massacre.

From the Old State House, leave the Freedom Trail and go to *Beaver II*, a replica of the smallest ship in the Boston Tea Party. On December 16, 1973, people relived the 200th anniversary of this important historical event. Some people dressed in colonial costumes and others disguised as Indians climbed aboard *Beaver II* and dumped chests of tea into the water.

You can climb aboard the ship and throw chests into the water, too, but they will not float away. These chests are tied to ropes and are pulled up again so the next person can throw them in. After you visit the ship and museum, get back on the Freedom Trail and head for Faneuil Hall.

An aerial view of the Faneuil Hall marketplace

Farmers sold their crops there. Peter Faneuil built a meeting hall above the stalls. He gave the building to Boston and said it must be used to help people. Because so many meetings were held in this hall, it is called the Cradle of Liberty.

Frederick Douglass and William Lloyd Garrison spoke against slavery in Faneuil Hall. Amelia Jenks Bloomer, one of the earliest women

A U.S. park ranger gives a talk inside Faneuil Hall.

to promote women's rights, spoke there also. Arguments for and against every American war have echoed throughout the hall. But meetings are not always about politics, human rights, and wars. There is an army museum at Faneuil Hall, and concerts are played there. Every year students come to Faneuil Hall for the city spelling bee.

Before you walk away from the hall, look at the weather vane shaped like a grasshopper. Made of copper and gold leaf, it is so big that Shem Drowne, the deacon who made it, used glass doorknobs for the grasshopper's eyes. It has been on the hall since 1742. During the War of 1812, it identified spies. If a person did not know the shape of the weather vane on Faneuil Hall, soldiers believed that person was a spy.

CHAPTER 4

SPIES AND A MIDNIGHT RIDE

The next Freedom Trail building is Paul Revere's house. It is the oldest building in Boston, but it is not the original house built on that land. In 1676 a fire destroyed 45 houses in the area, and the one you see today was built in 1680. Revere bought the house in 1770. He often walked to his shop two blocks away.

Revere was always ready to ride to deliver British secrets. When Dr. Joseph Warren asked him to warn other patriots that the British were on the move, he jumped at the chance to help. On the day before his famous ride, Revere rowed across the Charles River to Charlestown to tell people there was talk of an attack.

He borrowed a horse from Colonel William

Paul Revere's house. It is from this place that Revere began his famous ride.

Conant, and at Lexington Common, Revere passed the schoolhouse and the bells that warned patriots of fires and other dangers. Then he went to the Reverend Jonas Clark's parsonage to talk to Samuel Adams and John Hancock. They were surprised to see him, but they were not surprised to hear that the British planned to stop them from going to the Second Continental Congress.

From there, Revere rode to Concord, five miles away. For months, patriots had been melting spoons, teapots, pans, and nails to make bullets. They had been grinding charcoal and sulphur to make gunpowder. Minutemen also had tents, candles, axes, and boxes of medicine. Revere was glad to see that the men were ready.

While he rode back to Colonel Conant's house, Revere thought of ways to alert people when the British made their move. Someone could ride from Boston by land or row across the river. But if the British caught that person, there would be no warning. Revere found the answer to his problem at Colonel Conant's house.

Across the river, Paul Revere saw the steeple of Christ Church, the tallest in Boston. Within moments, he had thought of a plan. If the British attacked by land, there would be one light in the steeple. If they attacked by sea, there would be two. As he rowed back to Boston, Revere decided to ask the caretaker at Christ Church, Robert Newman, to give the signal. Newman agreed to put the signal in the steeple.

The next day, Dr. Warren told Revere that their spies had learned that hundreds of boats were in the water near the Common. British soldiers were seen marching toward the boats. Then Dr. Warren said William Dawes was racing overland to warn people, but with British soldiers everywhere, he might not get there. Revere said he would cross the river. One of them must get through. Then he hurried to tell Robert Newman to put two lanterns in the steeple.

Revere found the caretaker searching for him. Newman said his house was filled with British soldiers and he had to sneak out of his bedroom window. Revere worried about Robert Newman getting back to his room without being seen. He was also concerned about the caretaker climbing the stairs to the steeple.

When Paul Revere was 15, he had climbed the same stairs once a week to ring the bells for two hours.

Revere told Robert Newman the safest way to get up the stairs was to keep his hand against the wall to feel the twists and turns. Then Revere told the caretaker to hold the lanterns far apart so lookouts across the river would know the British were attacking by sea. He said to let the lanterns shine for only a moment so the British would not see the flames.

Two of Revere's friends risked their lives to row him across the river. The British had orders to stop any patriots who tried to cross. When the rowboat got close to a ship, the men stopped rowing, so the sailors would not hear the oars in the water. The boat drifted past and then the men rowed again.

On shore, Revere was relieved when Colonel Conant said he'd seen the signal in the steeple. Revere was glad, too, that Deacon John Larkin had offered his best horse. But there was bad news, too. British soldiers filled the countryside. It was dangerous to ride to Lexington, but Paul Revere had to give the warning. He raced away on the deacon's horse.

When Revere spotted British soldiers, he raced his horse and left them behind. In Medford he woke up the captain of the Minutemen, Isaac Hall. Then he shouted at every farmhouse on the way to Lexington. Within moments, people fired muskets, beat drums, and rang bells to alert others. Boys too young to fire muskets jumped on their horses to spread word of the attack.

After Revere had finished telling Samuel Adams and John Hancock the news, William Dawes arrived. He had reached Lexington by bribing British soldiers. Now the men had to warn people in Concord. Halfway there, soldiers arrested them. William Dawes and Samuel Prescott, a friend they met on the way, escaped. But an officer held a gun to Paul Revere's head

and took him prisoner.

On the way back to Lexington, Revere worried he would be shot or sent to England and hanged as a traitor. He was looking for a chance to escape when a shot rang out at the Common. His guards decided they could escape from the Minutemen faster without a prisoner: They let Revere go. But they kept Deacon Larkin's horse, and Revere had to walk to the parsonage.

He got there after four o'clock. Then he, Samuel Adams, and John Hancock and his secretary started for Woburn. They rode a couple of miles before John Hancock remembered he had left secret records in Lexington. Revere and the secretary went back to get the trunk. There they saw hundreds of British soldiers marching toward the Lexington Common.

A shot rang out. Paul Revere turned to see who had fired. He saw smoke rise in front of some British soldiers. Then he saw them rush toward the Minutemen, and he heard more gun-

A portrait of Paul Revere

fire. The first shots of the Revolutionary War had been fired.

While Paul Revere's life was in danger, so was Robert Newman's. He took the lanterns he had hidden under the stairs in the belfry. Then he climbed more stairs to the top. Revere had said to hold the lanterns apart and to hold them only a moment. But how far was far enough? And how long was a moment? Robert Newman prayed, then lit the lanterns, held them at the window, and quickly blew out the flames.

Then he guided himself down the stairs with his hand against the wall. He wanted to run so he could get home before the soldiers found out he was not in his room. But there were too many twists in the stairs. On the way down, he heard voices. He stopped. He heard voices again. It was too dangerous to go out the door, so he climbed out a window and ran home. Then he went through his upstairs window and lay in bed, unable to sleep.

Robert Newman did not get much sleep after he was arrested, either. The British asked him question after question. But he convinced them he had not put the lanterns in the steeple. He was released and then he left Boston.

Revere left Boston, too. It was too dangerous to stay in his house on North Street. His wife, Rachel, and his children went to live with him in Watertown. His oldest son, Paul, stayed in Boston to protect the house from British soldiers.

Christ Church was built in 1723. It has not changed much since Robert Newman climbed to the steeple. The brass chandeliers, the organ, and the clock are still used. And you can see the window from which the caretaker escaped.

CHAPTER 5

THE WHITES OF
THEIR EYES

Not far from Old North Church is Copp's Hill Burial Ground. British soldiers camped there and sometimes used the gravestones for target practice. On June 17, 1775, they fired their cannons on Charlestown and burned the city down during the Battle of Bunker Hill.

Robert Newman is buried in the cemetery. More than a thousand African Americans who lived at the bottom of Copp's Hill are also buried there. One of them is Prince Hall. He earned his freedom by fighting in the Continental Army. After the Revolutionary War, Prince Hall started Boston's first school for African American children.

Your next stop is Charlestown Navy Yard.

Copp's Hill Burial Ground

There you can see the USS *Constitution*. It was launched in 1797 to protect American ships from British and French ships and from pirates.

The *Constitution*, the oldest ship in the U.S. Navy, was nicknamed "Old Ironsides" because cannon balls bounced off its hull. The ship never lost a battle and helped the United States win the War of 1812. By 1830 the *Constitution* was in such bad shape it was ordered destroyed. But

Each year, on July 4, the USS Constitution *sails through Boston harbor.*

after poet Oliver Wendell Holmes praised the ship in his poem "Old Ironsides," people insisted the ship be saved.

Guides dressed in 19th-century naval uniforms take you through the *Constitution* and tell stories of the ship's battles and courageous crews. The *Constitution* sails once a year. On the Fourth of July, tugboats push it through the harbor while thousands of people cheer from shore.

Close by is a museum where you can swing in a sailor's hammock, raise a sail, and turn the steering wheel. You can walk around a platform that used to be 90 feet above a deck. Imagine you are up there on a stormy night watching for ships, while the platform rocks and shakes in the wind.

From the *Constitution*, go to the Bunker Hill Pavilion to see the sound-and-light show that brings the Battle of Bunker Hill to life. The battle was supposed to be fought on Bunker Hill. But on April 16, Minutemen worked all night with dirt, wood, and rocks to build forts on nearby Breed's Hill. Captain William Prescott decided to fight there.

In the morning, when British soldiers saw the makeshift forts, General Thomas Gage told his men they would quickly scatter the Minutemen. Then his soldiers could sweep through the countryside. Since this would take about three days, the soldiers decided to bake bread and cook meat for their sweep. While the British cooked, the Minutemen worked on their forts. By the time the British got around to fighting, the Minutemen were ready.

The British marched in rows, barely breaking ranks, even when they reached the walls, fences, and anything else the Minutemen had put in the way. To save ammunition, the Minutemen had been told, "Do not fire till you see the whites of their eyes." Because no bullets came at them, the British believed the Minutemen were cowards. Then the British heard a word echo over the hill: "Fire!" Rows of British soldiers fell dead or wounded.

The British tried again. The Minutemen fired again. Finally, with their bullets running out, the Minutemen retreated. Many of them had been killed, including Dr. Joseph Warren, who had sent Paul Revere on his midnight ride.

Dedicated in 1843, the Bunker Hill Monument is near the place Dr. Warren died. When the battle was fought, Breed's Hill was covered with pastures. Now, like the rest of the Freedom Trail, it is surrounded by buildings.

Climb the 294 steps to the top of the monument. From there you can see Boston. It is not the Boston Paul Revere and other patriots saw. But if you close your eyes, you may be able to imagine the patriots who fought so hard for their freedom. And if you imagine really hard, you may hear the shot Paul Revere heard on Lexington Common. It was called the shot heard around the world.

The Constitution *in its dock, with the Bunker Hill Monument in the background*

VISITOR INFORMATION

(All sites, except USS *Constitution*, are closed
Thanksgiving, Christmas, and New Year's Day.
Information may change without notice. Visitors are
advised to call beforehand.)

Boston Common—Starting point for the Freedom
Trail, (617) 536-4100. Monday to Saturday 8:30 to
5:00; Sunday, 9:00 to 5:00. Open year-round.
Admission is free.

The Massachusetts State House—Beacon Street,
(617) 727-3676, Monday to Friday, 10:00 to 4:00,
closed weekends. Call ahead for group reservations.
Admission is free.

Granary Burial Ground—Tremont Street, next to
Park Street Church (corner of Park and Tremont
Streets), (617) 635-4505. Open daily during daylight
hours. Admission is free.

King's Chapel—Corner of School and Tremont Streets,
(617) 523-1749. Spring and summer hours: Tuesday
to Saturday, 10:00 to 4:00; winter hours: Tuesday to
Friday, 10:00 to 2:00, Saturday 10:00 to 4:00.
Donations requested.

Old South Meeting House—Corner of Washington and
Milk Streets, (617) 482-6439. April through October,
daily 9:30 to 5:30; November through March,
Monday through Friday: 10:00 to 4:00, weekends:

10:00 to 5:00. Admission: $2.50 adults, $1.00 children (6-18), $2.00 senior citizens and students.

Old State House—Corner of State and Washington Streets, (617) 720-3290. Admission: $2.00 adults, 75 cents for children ages 6 to 18, $2.00 senior citizens and students.

Boston Massacre Site—On State Street next to Old State House. See the circle of cobblestones.

Faneuil Hall—Congress Street at Quincy Market, (617) 635-3105. Open daily 9:00 to 5:00. Admission is free.

Paul Revere House—19 North Square, North End, (617) 523-2338. November 1 through April 14, 9:30 to 4:15; April 15 through October 31, 9:30 to 5:15. Closed Mondays January through March. Admission: Adults $2.50, children $1.00, children under 5 free, students and seniors $2.00.

USS *Constitution*—Charlestown Navy Yard, (617) 742-0543. Open daily 9:30 to 5:30 for guided tours, 3:50-sunset for self-guided top deck tours. Admission is free.

HISTORICAL TIME LINE

1630 Colonists land in Massachusetts and settle in Boston.

1632 Boston becomes the capital of the Massachusetts Bay Colony.

1765 Stamp Act passed. People in Boston riot against it.

1766 Stamp Act repealed. People celebrate.

1768 October 1, British soldiers are sent to keep peace in Boston.

1770 February 22, Christopher Snider is killed by British soldiers.

1770 March 5, the Boston Massacre takes place.

1773 December 16, patriots throw tea from British ships. The event is called the Boston Tea Party.

1774 Patriots organize the Minutemen.

1774 September 5, First Continental Congress meets in Philadelphia.

1775 April 18, Paul Revere and William Dawes warn the patriots that the British are marching to Charlestown.

1775 June 17, Battle of Bunker Hill is fought.

1776 July 18, the Declaration of Independence is read from the balcony of the Old State House.

1797 The USS *Constitution* is launched.

1843 The Bunker Hill Monument is dedicated.

INDEX

Adams, Samuel, 18, 20, 29, 32, 34, 43, 47, 49
African Americans, 26, 28, 52
Attucks, Crispus, 14, 38

Battle of Bunker Hill, 52, 56
Beacon Hill, 24, 28, 36
Black Heritage Trail, 28, 29
"Bloody Massacre," 16, 38
Boston Common, 11, 21, 24, 45
Boston harbor, 17, 18, 20, 24
Boston Massacre 8, 16, 17, 38
Boston Tea Party, 8, 18, 19, 38
Breed's Hill, 57, 58
British soldiers, 8, 11, 12, 13, 14, 16, 21, 26,
    32, 34, 36, 42, 43, 44, 45, 46, 47, 49, 51,
    52, 57, 58
Bunker Hill, 21
Bunker Hill Monument, 58
Bunker Hill Pavilion, 56

Charles River, 9, 42
Charlestown, Massachusetts, 8-9, 24, 42, 52
Charlestown Navy Yard, 9, 52, 53
Christ Church, 44, 45, 51
Civil War, 8, 26
Clark, Reverend Jonas, 43
Conant, Colonel William, 42, 43, 44, 46
Concord, Massachusetts, 21, 44, 47
Continental Army, 52
Copp's Hill Burial Ground, 52
Cradle of Liberty, 39
Crafts, Colonel Thomas, 37
Custom House, 13, 14, 16

Dawes, William, 31, 45, 47
Declaration of Independence, 37
Douglass, Frederick, 39

England, 9, 11, 12, 17, 20, 37, 49

Faneuil Hall, 11, 38, 39, 40, 41
First Continental Congress, 20
Fort Wagner, 28
Franklin, Benjamin, 29, 32
Frog Pond, 24

Gage, General Thomas, 20, 57
Garrison, William Lloyd, 39

Granary Burying Ground, 13, 16, 29, 30
Griffin's Wharf, 18

Hancock, John, 18, 20, 29, 32, 43, 47, 49
Holmes, Oliver Wendell, 56
Hutchinson, Governor Thomas, 12, 17, 18,
    36

king of England, 9, 11, 12, 17, 20, 21, 24, 36
King's Chapel Burial Ground, 30, 31, 32
King's Chapel, 32, 34

Larkin, Deacon John, 46, 47, 49
Lexington, Massachusetts, 7, 21, 31, 47, 49
Lexington Common, 43, 49, 58
Longfellow, Henry W., 7, 32

Massachusetts Assembly, 37
Massachusetts Bay Colony, 9, 20, 24, 36
Massachusetts State House, 24, 26
Minutemen, 21, 44, 47, 49, 56, 57, 58

Newman, Robert, 45, 46, 50, 51, 52

Old North Church, 52
Old State House, 36, 37, 38

patriots, 11, 12, 17, 18, 19, 20, 26, 32, 34, 37,
    42, 43, 44, 46, 58
Philadelphia, 19, 20, 29
Preston, Captain Thomas, 14, 16

Revere, Paul, 7, 8, 9, 16, 18, 19, 21, 29, 31,
    32, 42, 43, 44, 45, 46, 47, 49, 50, 51, 58
Revolutionary War, 34, 50, 52

Second Continental Congress, 21, 44
Shaw, Colonel Robert Gould, 26, 27, 28
Snider, Christopher, 12, 13

Tories, 11, 12, 32, 34, 37

USS *Constitution* ("Old Ironsides"), 8, 9,

War of 1812, 9, 29, 41, 53
Warren, Dr. Joseph, 42, 45, 58
World War II, 26

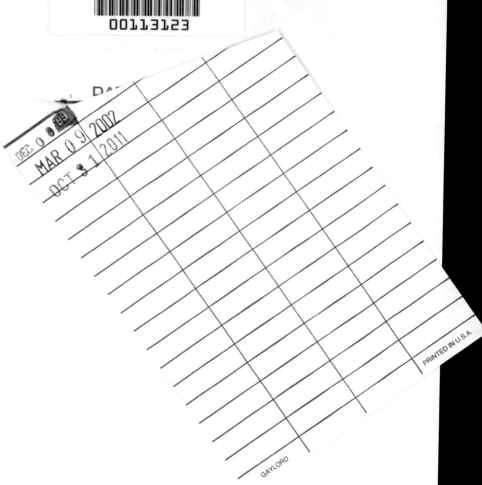